THE CLASSROOM
THE LIFE AND TIMES OF A TEACHER

MELVINA ELDORA SAMUEL

CONTENTS

Acknowledgments	v
Dedication	vii
Overview	1
Introduction	3
1. My Childhood Years 1961 - 1973	6
2. My Home Life	13
3. My Teaching Years 1973 - 1978	19
4. My Teaching Years 1978 - 1995	24
5. My Principal Years 1995 - 2005	29
6. Teaching in Texas at the Early Childhood Level 2009 - 2023	35
7. Motherhood	39
8. Poems Written by Melvina Samuel	42
About the Author	53

Copyright © 2026 Melvina Eldora Samuel

All rights reserved. No part of this publication may be reproduced, distributed, or transmitted in any form or by any means, including photocopying, recording, or other electronic or mechanical methods, without the prior written permission of the publisher, except in the case of brief quotations embodied in critical reviews and certain other noncommercial uses permitted by copyright law.

ISBN: 979-8-218-90829-4

ACKNOWLEDGMENTS

To the Great Teacher, Almighty God, who has blessed me tremendously over the past years of my life. In His classroom, I have learned many lessons that have guided and shaped my life. To Him be the Glory.

The Classroom started many years ago. There were seasons of delay, discouragement, and procrastination. However, by the grace of God, it has been brought to fruition.

To my niece, Dr. Trecia Arthurton, who helped me push beyond my self-doubt, and whose determination and guidance helped me to realize that it can be done.

To my daughter, Carelle Samuel Osborne, whose critique was invaluable in getting the job done.

To my family, thank you for all your support.

To all the children who sat in my classrooms over the years, thank you for making me the teacher I am today.

To all the teachers with whom I collaborated over the years, thank you

To all who will read this book, thank you, and may you have a rich learning experience in The Classroom.

DEDICATION

The Classroom is dedicated to the memory of my mother, Veronica "Vie" Stevens. Momma Vie, as she was affectionately called, was the bedrock of my success as a teacher. A single mother of seven, she was an entrepreneur par excellence who plied her trade of selling black pudding by pushing her cart from one end of Basseterre to another.

As the years went by, she expanded her trade to include the selling of fruits, drinks, baked goods, and toys in the market, as well as walking around Basseterre. She also sold bananas and oranges early in the morning.

Sometimes it was on her return from these daily sales that dinner would begin, as she depended on her sales to feed her children.

Momma would always emphasize, "Go to school and take in your education, because I don't want you to be out like me selling black pudding." This stuck with me and was the driving force for me to succeed in school. She always ensured that we attended school dressed and had everything we needed to succeed. She was our seamstress and ensured that our clothes for church and school were nicely made. I can still see her making our clothes during the weeks leading up to the reopening of school, most times doing her sewing after she had done her day's selling.

Her sacrifices and devotion to her children were exemplary. I recall in 1973 that my sister Carmen and I were going to sit our GCE exams. She said, "Where am I going to get so much money to pay for these exams?" In December of 1972, during the Carnival season, she answered her own question. She decided to set up a stall at the corner of Fort Street and Cayon Street, next to what was called Seaton's Drug Store at the time. During the Carnival Season, she sold bottled drinks and black pudding. This venture was so successful that it gave her all the money she needed to pay for our exams. As a result, she continued doing this every year and expanded her products to include candies. She continued this until she retired from selling in 2004

On the day we went to school to collect our GCE exam results, she did not leave for her selling until we came home with the results. She was incredibly happy when she heard we had passed our subjects. She was extremely proud when I became a teacher and my sister became a nurse. She felt a sense of accomplishment. She was proud that she had a teacher and a nurse, something that had evaded her. She felt complete.

After retirement, she moved to the United States and enjoyed life there, returning to St. Kitts every Christmas. She enjoyed living with her children, Centilia and Olive, and her many grandchildren who came to visit her from time to time. On Saturday, April 13, 2019, she passed away in Tampa, Florida. Her funeral service was held at the Zion Moravian Church on Monday, April 29, at the Zion Moravian Church in Basseterre. She is buried in Springfield Cemetery in St. Kitts.

Momma Vie is the woman who taught me how to be a committed and dedicated teacher and how to nurture the young children in my care.

OVERVIEW

Growing up in humble beginnings in the Caribbean island of St. Kitts in the 1960s, my life was simple, idyllic, and exciting. We did not have much, but we were happy, satisfied, and lived a comfortable life. It was my childhood dream to be a teacher, as I tried to emulate some of the teachers I experienced in my young life. I would always think about my childhood teachers and play school at every opportunity.

When this dream was realized at the age of 17, I was ecstatic but timid. I was ecstatic that my dream was now becoming a reality, and timid because I did not feel that I was competent to do the job. I was a shy 17-year-old who showed up at St. Johnston Village School (now called the Dr. William Connor Primary School) on the morning of Monday, October 1, 1973.

The Classroom tells my life story, the failures and successes of my teaching career. It tells of my classroom experiences as a young child, and also my experiences as a classroom teacher, and my lessons learned in the classroom of life. I want to encourage young readers to realize that no matter where you start, you can finish strong. I want to encourage them and help them realize that they, too, can pursue their dreams and be whatever they want to be.

At a time when it is difficult to get people to pursue a career in teaching, when the teaching profession is no longer the cherished profession it once was, I wish through this book to encourage young people to pursue this career, as it is a rewarding one.

Seeing a young three-year-old write his or her name for the first time brings joy that cannot be explained. Hearing a young child read a book after you helped him with words is a great feeling of accomplishment. Just seeing the children you teach taking their rightful place in society today is extremely satisfying. The little children who once sat in classrooms are now in charge of institutions and making decisions that affect the lives of others.

Whenever I visit home, it gives me immense pleasure to walk into a bank, hospital, store, supermarket, church, construction site, hotel, or school and see children who once sat in my classroom taking their rightful place in society. Many are medical doctors, and many who migrated are also fulfilling their role in their part of the world. Being invited out to dinner by children who once sat in my classroom and hearing their admiration of the effect I had on their lives often makes me thankful that I chose teaching as my career.

Today, many of my students hold executive positions in their chosen careers. I am extremely proud to know that one of my students, Dr. Terrance Drew, is now the Prime Minister of St. Kitts and Nevis. Another is the principal of the Deane Glasford Primary School, a position I once held.

INTRODUCTION

"I touch the future; I teach."

Never has this saying become more real to me than in April 2008, when I visited my home country of St. Kitts, located in the Eastern Caribbean, after being absent from there for a period of three years.

In almost every institution I visited, I met children whom I had taught at some level during my career. There were tellers in all the banks, namely Bank of Nova Scotia, St. Kitts Nevis National Bank, Royal Bank of Canada, and the St. Kitts Credit Union. I met my past students as cashiers in supermarkets, as construction workers working on buildings, those who are now medical practitioners, as nurses in the hospitals and Health Centers, as well as doctors and technicians in the hospital. I also encountered clerks in places like TDC, Horsford's, and Delisle Walwyn. I was most delighted to find many of those who walked in my footsteps and became teachers. Within the church, there were my past students who were very active, serving in various capacities.

As I looked at these students, I reflected on the days I

encountered these children and what I did to promote them and give them the foundations they need to be performing at this level today. Looking at them made me realize that when touching the life of a young child, it is very important that teachers take their role seriously. My advice to teachers in today's world:

1. Treat your children with respect.
Children will respect you if they realize you respect them. I never fail to say sorry to a child if I accidentally bump into them or if I accuse them of something, then realize that was not the case. I always give children a chance to tell their side of the story.

2. Show them love.
Children adore teachers. They believe what teachers tell them and are willing to take their advice at times. I have realized that many times, the children we teach lack love, no matter the social setting of their home. Showing love to children goes a long way.

3. Imagine that they are your own children.
This is something I always bear in mind each time I come in contact with children.

4. Prepare your lessons to accommodate the children you teach.
Sometimes, because we are a society geared to preparing children for tests, we tend to overlook the individualities of the children and push on to teach for the tests. Teachers should take into consideration the children they teach when preparing lessons.

5. Do not waste children's time.
Children should receive maximum attention when they are in the classroom. The time spent in the classroom should not be wasted.

6. Be creative.
Encourage children to have a love for learning. When planning lessons, teachers should realize that children are inquisitive by nature. Plan lessons that satisfy their curiosity. Children today are born in the technological age. Teachers should make use of technology in teaching in today's world.

Teachers, always remember, you touch the future, you teach. Remember this each time you stand in front of a class. Remember that someday these kids will stand where you are now. Yes, teachers, you are important in the lives of these children. Take your job seriously. It is one of those jobs where the income is small, but I can assure you that the outcome is priceless.

CHAPTER 1
MY CHILDHOOD YEARS
1961 - 1973

I often wondered what the weather and living conditions were on Sunday, August 5, 1956, when I was born to a single mother in Happy Hill Alley, New Town, Basseterre, St. Kitts. I was the third child born to her on that day. In those days, mothers had their babies at home and were delivered by midwives.

I grew up in the eastern area of Basseterre, St. Kitts, known as New Town. I recall living in a small two-room house on George Street during my early years. To this day, I still wonder how a family of seven could live in such a small environment. I lived in an extended family that included my mother, my grandmother, my great aunt, and my four siblings at that time. My mother would go on to have seven more children, four of whom died at birth. Life for me as a young child was simple. It was here, though, that my love for teaching began.

I recall playing school as the teacher, using the trees around as the students. I would always have books and use charcoal as chalk. I recall playing outside in the evening with other children in the neighborhood, and when it was

9:00 p.m., we had to end play, say our goodbyes, and head for the house. We would know it was 9:00 p.m. by the blowing of the horn from the sugar factory. We had no television, video games, tablet, or cell phones in those days, so we played outside.

When I was eight years old, my family moved from New Town to Irish Town, and we resided at West Bourne Street. Here, the house was much larger than my previous residence. However, I did not like the area of Irish Town. It was my wish that we not move from the community of New Town. Growing up in St. Kitts during the late 60s and early 70s, life was very simple.

We did not have much, but we were very happy. I attended school at New Town Primary School, now renamed Tucker Clarke Primary School. The school was first located on the corner of Sandown Road and Pond Road. Classes were also held in some buildings on Ponds Pasture.

When I was in Grade 3, the school moved to its present location on Ponds Pasture. This was a happy moment as we made the move to that location. I proudly remember my teachers from that era. I was always in awe of my teachers, looking at their style of teaching, the way they dressed, and the way they interacted with their students. I am convinced that this is the time and era in which the decision was made that I would be a teacher. As young children, we would always categorize our teachers as those who were friendly, those who were "hoggish," those who liked to beat, and those who could and couldn't teach.

For as long as I could remember, Christine Tucker was always the headmistress. She was the head teacher up to the time I became a teacher, and she congratulated me on choosing that career. Ms. Tucker was a serious and dedicated head teacher who was a disciplinarian and who instilled many values in her students. She took the time to be present at every morning assembly, teaching us the hymns of faith, using the tonic solfa—something I do not understand to this day. She always gave us lectures on behavior, deportment, how to speak properly, and other facts of life. Ms. Tucker was well respected by the members of the community. New Town Primary School is today named in her honor, in addition to another headteacher, Dorothy Clarke, who came after her. It is now called Tucker Clarke Primary School.

I still remember the teachers I had during my years at New Town Primary School. Most have since passed on to their eternal home:

- Kindergarten: Ms. Ash
- Grade 1: Teacher Vassil Richards
- Grade 2: Ms. Beryl Lawrence
- Grade 3: Ms. Ethlyn White
- Grade 4: Teacher Cynthia Fielding
- Grade 5: Ms. Janet Nisbett
- Grade 6: Ms. Theresa Richardson

During that time, New Town Primary School was always a force to reckon with. I recalled that I represented the school in an interschool quiz at Basseterre Boys School. The schools represented were Basseterre Boys, Basseterre Girls, Irish Town, and St. Johnston Village School. Our school was victorious. New Town Primary School was also the first primary school on the island to organize an interhouse school sports meet.

The school was a beacon in the community of New Town. That everyone admired. Teachers during this time were very strict. The strap was a dominant feature in every classroom. The headmistress also had a strap, and it seemed she carried it with her wherever she went on the school grounds. Teachers then were in full control of their classrooms. The bell rang at 9:00 a.m., and you had to be on time for school.

The morning began with the morning assembly. However, before you entered the school, you were met at the gate by the headmistress, who was conducting her inspection. Inspection meant that you had to show your teeth, nails, and hair and make sure they were clean before you could enter the school. If they were not clean, you felt the strap, or sometimes she would give you a pass with some words of advice. You also had to ensure that you were early for school. This was not done daily, but it was done regularly. By doing this, Ms. Tucker instilled in us at a young age the importance of punctuality and cleanliness. Lessons I appreciate and hold dear to this day.

Morning assembly consisted of the singing of hymns and prayers. It was at school that I learned hymns like "When I Survey the Wondrous Cross" and "The Lord's My Shepherd." "The Day thouavest Lord is Ended." She would use the tonic solfa, and we had to sing do, re, mi, fa, so, la, ti, do before singing the songs. In those days, we prayed three times a day at school. We prayed in the morning, before going for lunch, and before going home in the afternoon. The classroom really laid the foundation for Christian living.

As I recall, the method of teaching used in those days was "chalk and talk." Everything was written on the chalkboard, and you had to pay close attention to what the teachers were saying. In mathematics, which was called "arithmetic" at that time, teachers worked examples on the board. Then, it was your turn to go to the board and work on an example. Following that, you were given several examples to work on your own.

In the sixth grade, mental arithmetic was given every day. This was an activity where the teacher would read math problems, and you had to solve them mentally and write the answer only. The foundation for my reading and spelling ability was laid right here at New Town Primary School. Teachers would set the pace for reading by modeling how the passage should be read. You were then called upon to read the same passage. Spelling was given every Friday. You were given the words to study during the week, and some of those words formed the test on Friday.

Books were always available for reading, and I loved to read. I recall having won a fairy tale book for a prize at school. I would read that book even while walking to the shop. One day, while walking, I was so engrossed in reading the book that I was almost hit by a car.

When the school relocated to Ponds Pasture, there were no houses on the pasture as there are today. Therefore, as children, we played among the bushes on the pasture as well as on the playfield close by. In those days, we got recess two times per day, one in the morning and one in the afternoon. Recess on Friday afternoons lasted from 2:00 until 3:15 when school ended. We looked forward to playing among the bushes on Ponds Pasture.

One of the features of school life at that time was when the nurses visited the school to give what we called injections. Those were days when the nurses from the Basseterre Health Center would visit the school and give vaccinations. There would be screaming from those children who were scared of the vaccinations, stories of the nurse who threw the needle in their hand. Those who went in for their vaccination would give you advice as to which nurse not to go to because they were rough and would make your hand hurt.

Another memorable feature of school life was scrubbing the wooden desks on the last day of school at the end of each school term. Students would bring their scrubbing brushes, soap, and rags to scrub the desks. Those who did not have brushes used the plants nearby to scrub the desks. This was a really enjoyable activity for us as children. We enjoyed splashing in the water as we cleaned the desks and competed to see whose desk was cleaner.

When we moved from New Town to Irish Town in 1964, my siblings and I continued attending school at New Town Primary instead of relocating to Irish Town Primary School. My mother resisted every effort to have us attend that school, as she considered New Town School the best school ever. I was delighted that we did not have to move from that school. During that time, owning a car was not on our horizon. It was not even a thought, so we walked to and from school daily from Irish Town to New Town. We walked to school in the morning, then home for lunch, and back to school, then home again in the evening.

In 1968, I sat the entrance exam to enter Girls High School. I knew with all my heart that I had aced that exam. However, I did not succeed in going to Girls' High School. It was the time in our history when entrance to that school hung heavily on your socio-economic status in society. As a result of that, I attended Basseterre Senior School for one year. This school was located on East Park Range. One year later, the education system was changed, and everyone had the right to attend high school. At that time, I was transferred to Basseterre Senior High School, where I attended from Form 2 to Form 5.

I was not prepared for the transition from Primary to

Secondary School. Life was different. Classes were larger; teachers were different. There was one teacher for every subject. You had to relate to people you had never met before. Fitting into this new environment was a challenge for me.

As I reflect on my life, I am convinced that New Town Primary School laid the foundation for my love for reading and my love for teaching. I left this school in 1968 and returned ten years later in 1977 to perform my final teaching practice during my years as a student teacher at the St. Kitts Teachers' Training College.

CHAPTER 2
MY HOME LIFE

I grew up in an extended family setting. I lived with my mother, whom we called Momma Vi, her mother (my grandmother), whom we called Momma Freda, and my great aunt, whom we called Aunty. There were seven of us as children: Kenneth, Carmen, Olive, Hillario, Franco, and Centilia.

My mother was a seamstress who made our clothes until we started working, when she instructed us to go out and buy our clothes or get someone else to make them.

She was also a street vendor, made black pudding, and traveled the streets of Basseterre to sell her pudding on weekdays. She traveled from Irish Town to New Town every day except on Thursdays, selling her pudding. She would settle at New Town Bay Road in the area facing Herbert Street, then walk the journey back to Irish Town. On our journey home from New Town School, we would stop at that spot and then make our journey home.

My mother was known for her black pudding and selling skills. She would get all her materials for the pudding from the Public Market. Life was busy on a

Saturday when she made most of the pudding. Everyone had to be involved in getting the job done. This included getting the stuff from the Public Market to the house, making the pudding, and getting it to the point of sale. As we were at school, we did not assist with the daily making of the pudding from Monday to Friday, but Saturday was an extremely busy day from morning to evening.

Early in the morning, we had to go to the Public Market located on the Irish Town Bay Road to gather the materials, then back home to assist with the making. This was hard work as we had to make it, then clean up after it was done. On most Saturdays, we had to make extra pudding as the sales were quick, and she would finish what she had and demanded that more be made. I hardly had a social life on a Saturday, as we were expected to work at home. Growing up, we were taught to work hard.

Apart from Saturday work with the pudding, we as girls were expected to wash, cook, iron clothes, and clean the house. There was no washing machine in our house in those days. I had to wash the clothes by hand in a bath-pan using a washing board, soap powder, and a scrubbing brush to help remove the tough stains.

Life was good. We always had what we needed, whether it was clothes or food, but my love for clothes made me believe that I did not have enough clothes. We attended church on most Sundays at the Zion Moravian Church. My mother made our clothes, and she always gave us a new dress for Easter, Harvest Festival, and Christmas. This was a must. Sunday dinner was always special. It consisted of rice and meat, vegetables, and macaroni pie. The meat and vegetables were all purchased at the Public Market. There were three great cooks in the family: my mother, my grandmother, and my great aunt.

An interesting feature for me growing up was the way we celebrated Christmas. My grandmother was regarded as the "accountant" of the family. She controlled the way the finances were to be spent. She held a tight economic rein on money from January to November. As December approached, she went all out to ensure that we had everything we needed for Christmas: toys, new clothes, food, and new furnishings for the house. During the first week of December, we had to practically strip the house, take the glasses out of the cabinet, wash them, and put them in a bath-pan. There was a flurry to paint the house every year, buy new curtains, varnish the old furniture, and sometimes replace it. It was always busy during the weeks leading up to Christmas Day.

Sorrel had to be picked and set up in a large bucket. Raisins, cherries, currants, and prunes were put to soak in wine weeks in advance for the making of the rum cake.

Christmas Eve was an extremely busy day at home. It was on this day that my mother would make a large amount of pudding, as sales were busy. As many people returned home from overseas for Christmas, the demand for pudding at this time of the year was great. Christmas Eve was the time when I worked around the clock. At the end of sales, you then had to "put out the house," as my mother would say. This included putting down the new linoleum in the days when we used linoleum, hanging the curtains, polishing the furniture, putting the glasses back into the cabinet, and generally making sure the house had a brand-new look.

Christmas Day was highly anticipated. There was always a lot of food—ham, chicken, meat, rice, macaroni pie, potato salad, sweet potato, collard greens, vegetables, fruit cake, plain cake, sorrel, ginger beer, soft drink, malt, beer, wine, liquor for the adults, cake, coconut tarts, and pies. On Christmas Day, we ate from the beginning of the day to the end of the day. One thing that stands out for me was the fact that I could not eat lunch on Christmas Day until I had taken the food for an old friend of my grandmother who lived alone and was disabled.

Another feature that stands out to me as a child is my social life, which was not much. I lived in an environment where discipline was strict, and we were limited as to where we could go. We could attend any function the church was having, as well as any function being held by the St. Kitts Labour Party. In those days, the primary school hardly had any function apart from a school fair. This we were allowed to attend. When we attended high school, we could not even attend Queen Shows or school dances, much to our disappointment. Our home was ruled with an iron fist, and all three adults in the home had the same way of thinking when it came to us attending functions.

I thoroughly enjoyed Easter Monday, because that was the day we would all gather in a bus with a neighbor, Ms. Sprouse, and her family and journey to Frigate Bay for a family picnic. This was an exciting time for us.

In those days, Queen's Birthday was celebrated on the second Saturday in June. That was the day we attended the Moravian Sunday School outing. This was an outing that was anticipated by all Moravians. As children, we had no vehicles of our own, so occasions such as going on a picnic enabled us to journey into the countryside in some large trucks or buses that provided transportation in those days. Those types of trucks are extinct today.

Going on these outings was fun. You got up early in the morning because you were so excited you could not sleep. No one had to wake you up this Saturday morning. All kinds of delicacies were prepared for taking to the picnic. All the food was packed into bags, and we traveled with them to the Moravian Church to catch the truck.

On these picnics, we were accompanied by my aunt. These picnics were usually held on pastures and rotated each year among Brotherson's Estate, Caine's Pasture, or Willet's Estate. As we journeyed in the trucks, we sang songs most of the way. At the picnic, the church organized its sports day. This included flat races, three-legged races, and sack races. The highlight of these activities, though, was the bun-eating race, which my brother Kenneth dominated.

Another feature of my young life which I treasure was being a member of the 1st St. Kitts Girls' Brigade Company. Girls' Brigade is a Christian organization for young girls. The 1st St. Kitts Girls' Brigade Company was founded in 1961 by Ms. Gubi, the wife of the Moravian Minister at that time. I attended Girls Brigade as a child under the guidance of leaders such as Ms. Doris Lloyd, Captain, Ms. Julia Bass-Hodge, Ms. Esther Ralph, and Ms. Patricia Delacoudray. Girls' Brigade meeting was held on Wednesdays at 5:00 p.m. I looked forward to going to these meetings not only to learn about the Bible, but also to participate in art and craft activities, as well as games. This was the time you also got to leave the house with no questions asked. Being involved in the Girls' Brigade also allowed us to become actively involved in activities outside of Basseterre, again allowing us to travel in buses or trucks to the countryside.

Attending Sunday school was also a must growing up. I recalled the days when we attended Sunday school at the Olivet Gospel Hall in Irish Town. When we arrived from that one, we attended Moravian Sunday School in New Town, conducted by Ms. Clarice Richardson. Later, when we moved to Irish Town, we attended Sunday school at the

Irish Town Moravian Schoolroom, conducted by Mrs. Violet, Leader of Greenlands. When that Sunday school became nonexistent, we attended Sunday school at the Zion Moravian Church.

Growing up, we were not rich, but we had what we needed. I recall never going to sleep hungry. As stated earlier, I lived with my mother, her mother, and her mother's sister. These were three strong women. They were also great cooks, and I marvel at the way they could cook without following recipes. They combined food and gave you the tastiest dishes that you could dream of.

Throughout my childhood years, my dream was to become a teacher. I would play school with imaginary characters, find a piece of board for the blackboard, and use pieces of charcoal as my chalk. I always saw myself becoming a teacher one day. I imitated my teachers when playing school and mimicked everything they did.

CHAPTER 3
MY TEACHING YEARS
1973 - 1978

It was Monday, October 1, 1973. The sun shone brightly. I was 17 years old. After waiting to be called by the Ministry of Education since the opening of school in September of that same year, I was officially walking to St. Johnston Village School (now renamed Dr. William Connor Primary School) to begin my career as a teacher. I walked from my residence on Market Street, a scared young individual. My dream had become a reality, but was I prepared for this day? The joy was there, but there was some semblance of fear—fear of what it would be like. However, here I was.

I recall walking into the school and being introduced to the rest of the staff. Immediately, I felt like a lamb among wolves. I was the youngest person in that room. Everyone else had been there for many years. My first assignment was to be in the kindergarten class with the late Mrs. Alma Procope. Mrs. Procope was a teacher for many years. I recall an incident that to this day I reflect on, and this is the reason why, as a Head Teacher, I was always very sympathetic to young teachers on their first assignment.

Mrs. Procope's mother died within weeks of my joining the staff. She took time off, and I was left with over 30 kindergarteners. Even though I thought I knew what I was doing, I had no idea how to manage the situation. As I reflect, though, classroom control at that time was good. The children were well behaved, so I did not have that issue to deal with.

I remember for a Math activity, I put an example like this one on the board: 2+1=. I sat down at my desk and waited for the children to come up with the answer. Many times in my career, I look back at this with dismay. Children at this level have to be able to get a concept of sets of numbers before they can even put sets together to do addition. I look back on this and realize how wrong I was and wish that I had not done this.

After one year at kindergarten, I was transferred to Grade 3 the next year. I loved teaching at this grade and enjoyed an extremely good relationship with my students. Most of the girls looked up to me as a big sister. I taught for two years at Grade 3 level. I was extremely proud of my teaching in these two years, especially when I was commended by Mrs. Lusca Theophilus, a tutor of the St. Kitts Teachers College. She felt that my standard was high and recommended that a junior Grade 4 teacher next door be allowed to observe my teaching. In 1974, I attended the in-service program of the St. Kitts Teachers College for two years every other Friday of the school year.

In 1976, I began attending the St. Kitts Teachers College full-time. Previously, the College program was designed for teachers to attend training for two years every other Friday, then one year of full-time training. In 1976, that changed, and my group of students attended training for two years full-time, thus making our group the first to start this new arrangement. During that time, I studied the following subjects:

- English Language, taught by Mrs. Dorothy Martin
- The Teaching of Reading, under the tutelage of Mrs. Sylvia Mills
- Education, taught by Mr. Arthur Richardson and Mrs. Lusca Theophilus
- Mathematics, taught by Mr. Adolphus Halliday and Mr. Osmond Petty
- Social Studies, taught by Mr. Arthur Richardson
- General Science, taught by Mr. Milton Whittaker and Mr. Lincoln Carty
- Health, taught by Ms. Lauretta Evelyn
- Craft, taught by the late Ismay Burt
- Individual Study and Practice Teaching

During my first year, I did my practice teaching at Basseterre Girls School (now known as Beach Allen Primary School). I was assigned to Grade 2 with the late Ms. Maureen Shepherd as my co-operating teacher. My co-teacher was the late Mrs. Camelita Jones of Nevis.

In my second year, I did two teaching practices. Both were done at the New Town Primary School—one in Grade 3 and the other in Grade 4. There was no co-teacher for these teaching practices. At Grade 3, my co-operating teacher was the late Mrs. Francille Liburd, who was also a teacher at that school at the time I attended school there, and at Grade 4, the late Mrs. Hortense Hanley.

For my Individual Study, I researched the following: *The Effectiveness of Drama versus Storytelling in the*

Teaching of Social Studies, Grade 4, at the Irish Town Primary School. In this study, I compared lessons taught on a unit entitled "My Island." I divided the class into two groups. The experimental group was taught using the drama approach, and the control group was taught using a lecture/storytelling approach. The results showed that children taught using the drama approach gained higher scores on the assessments given than those who were taught using the lecture/storytelling approach.

In conducting this study, I taught lessons over six weeks at Irish Town Primary School. These lessons were extremely interesting, and the children were actively engaged in the activities. At the end of the six weeks, both groups were given the same test. My study was coordinated by the Social Studies lecturer at that time, Dr. Arthur Richardson.

During my two years at Teachers College, I met several people as college mates. This group of teachers included people like John White, who went on to become the Chief Education Officer; William Hodge, who went on to become Headmaster of St. Paul's Primary and Sandy Point High School, and also the Permanent Secretary in the Ministry of Education. Fellow college mates who went on to become Headteachers, like myself included Marion Chapman Lescot, Earlene Maynard, Daun Wattley Hazel. Yvette Wallace, Emilita Jordan, and Selma Dolphin Broadbelt. Verdensia Charles later became a lecturer at the St. Kitts Teachers College; Siefroy Philip also became a principal and a lecturer at the St. Kitts Teachers College; and Gloria Mills became a Guidance Counselor at Sandy Point High School.

Other classmates included Pearline Wilson Nisbett, Florence Pemberton, Juliette Proctor, Carmelita Jones,

Eulyn Ward, Lornette Roper, Margaret Rose Hanley, Doreta Rouse, Jacklyn Bowry Benjamin, Osmond Farrell, Bernadette Lawrence, Constance Richardson, Cynthia Maxwell, Lydia Daniel, Osmond Farrel, Jovil Rogers, Ingrid Browne Berridge, Jackie Bowry, Rhyllis Vasquez, Shirley Dore Wilkes, and Violet Clifton. Today, we are known as the Teachers College Cohort 1976–1978. We communicate today using WhatsApp in a group chat. Three members of that group, Carmelita Jones, Florence Pemberton, and Constance Richardson, have since passed away.

CHAPTER 4
MY TEACHING YEARS
1978 - 1995

After graduating from St. Kitts Teachers College in June 1978, I did not return to St. Johnston Village (Dr. William Connor Primary School). I was transferred to St. Peter's Primary School, which was renamed Deane-Glasford Primary School. I had thyroid surgery during the summer of 1978, and therefore, my attendance was delayed, and I did not make it to the school in St. Peter's for the reopening in September. I lived in Basseterre, and therefore I was not at all familiar with the community of St. Peter's, which is located to the north of Basseterre. I journeyed to St. Peter's on that first morning by bus.

I recall being very, very cautious and uncertain as I arrived at my destination that morning. I had received so many warnings about the community of St. Peter's. It was not highly considered as the place to be. My grandmother warned me to be careful, but past teachers didn't give much encouragement either. I recall one telling me, "Why did they send you up here?" Whenever I was asked, "Where will you be going now that you have graduated?" I was greeted with, "What? Why up there?" However, on arriving, I felt comfortable and remained there for the next twenty-seven (27) years. Mrs. Doris Glasford was the headmistress at that time, and in her absence, Ms. Martha Deane functioned as Head. Other teachers at that time included Dolly Liburd, Laverne McKoy, Antonio Christopher, Julie James, Joan Philip, and Shirley Rawlings. Over the years, other staff members joined, and we worked well together. This school became the bedrock of my teaching career. Seventeen years later, I would become the principal of this school.

The St. Peter's community is an agricultural community. When I arrived at the school in October 1978, I realized that attendance was low, as some parents kept their children at home to help them work "their ground," as they referred to the lots of land they farmed. The school was considered at that time to be non-performing. In conversation with Mrs. Doris Glasford, the Head Teacher at that time, she informed me that she was extremely concerned about the school's performance. She said this was due to low attendance as well as the lack of teacher performance. She informed me that she would place me at Grade 1 because she wanted the children to continue building on the foundation they got in kindergarten. Although I was not pleased with this decision, I gave in to her demand and taught Grade 1 from 1978 to 1988. Mrs. Glasford retired in 1985, and the new Headteacher, Mrs. Elizabeth Condell, kept me at that grade level for another three years before giving in to my request to teach Grade 3.

My first Grade 1 class consisted of 40 children. Most of them were slow learners. I remember grouping them into four groups and collaborating with them tremendously to help them improve their performance. My attitude was that

I was fresh from college and full of knowledge, and I could get the job done. I continued to see these children improve in their work. Even though the class was big, I was able to give individual instruction and attention to those who needed help.

During my early tenure at St. Peter's Primary School, I had the privilege of either initiating or assisting with several extracurricular activities. One of the innovations that my presence at St. Peter's brought to the school was the introduction of clubs. Each Thursday afternoon, the upper Grades 3 to 6 were divided into groups. I was responsible for the drama club, which was very exciting. Children rushed to attend sessions. I look back on this and often say I missed my opportunity to study drama at a higher level.

I recall in 1981 we presented the play *Ma Lambee*, which I had written from a story in the book *Sun's Eye*. I rewrote the story as a play, but those children took it as their own, and not only did they perform, but they also designed the props for the presentation. I remember boys like Brian Brooks, Brian Bass, Brian Tuckett, and others getting cardboard boxes and making the huts for the village. I remember Geraldine Walters doing an amazing job as Ma Lambee. It was truly remarkable the way the children took control of the production of the play. The play was performed at the Anglican Church Hall, and many people were in attendance. It was well received by all who attended.

As mentioned earlier, the St. Peter's community is a farming community. Therefore, it was no surprise to find a large school garden located at the back of the school. The Head Teacher at that time, Ms. Doris Glasford, was very knowledgeable about gardening, and therefore, she was always at the forefront of the school garden. However, this did not sit well with some parents, and they did not agree with their children working in the school garden. The school benefited financially from the proceeds of the garden. Classes were assigned to each grade from Grade 3 to Grade 6, and each class had an agriculture period on its timetable.

Crops grown during that time included lettuce, cabbage, peppers, eggplant, sorrel, watermelon, white potatoes, and sweet potatoes. Children were given some of these crops to take home to plant, as well as the produce when it was reaped. The school was successful in winning or placing in the School Garden Competition held in those times.

Another feature of the school was its involvement in the annual Children's Carnival. The very first year I began working at the school, I was placed in charge of Carnival. Year after year, the school participated and won several trophies over a period of time. The school also took part in sporting activities (football, cricket, and netball), but was usually not as successful in this area.

Another highlight was the first staging of a Miss St. Peter's Primary School Pageant in 1983. This was a big venture taken on by the staff at that time. Contestants were Miss Green House, Cindy Jones; Miss Red House, Marsha Harris; Miss Orange House, Deslyn Gumbs; Miss Blue House, Cindy Newton; and Miss Gold House, Jennifer Edmeade. This was a first-time experience, and it was also well organized and well executed. Miss Jennifer Edmeade was crowned Miss St. Peter's Primary. First runner-up was Miss Red House, Marsha Harris, and second runner-up was Miss Green House, Cindy Jones. We received high praise from all who attended and from the community.

Even though we "bumped heads" at that time, especially as the day approached, special mention must be made of the staff at that time who worked tirelessly to make sure that it was a success: Ms. Pearline Burke, who made the dresses; Shirley Rawlings, who chaperoned Gold House; Joan Philip, who chaperoned Red House; Juliette James, who chaperoned Blue House; Veronica Liburd, who chaperoned Orange House; and myself, who chaperoned Green House. Mrs. Doris Glasford, the Head Teacher, ably managed the preparations for the show.

In July 1985, Mrs. Glasford retired as Head Teacher of the school. It was a sad moment to see her go. She was that Head Teacher who really had the school at heart. It pained her to see teachers not take their work seriously and parents who showed very little or no concern. She would tell of accounts where she had to journey throughout the community to encourage parents to send their children to school. At that time, she said parents would keep them at home to help in the "ground." According to her, there was a great improvement in the school from my arrival in 1978 to her departure in 1985. There was also a tremendous improvement in the attendance at school. This resonated in good student performance, and the image of the school improved tremendously, even though some parents from the community opted to send their children to the schools in Basseterre.

On her departure, the new Head Teacher was Mrs. Elizabeth Condell. She worked as Head Teacher from July 1985 to July 1994. I worked with Mrs. Condell as her deputy during this time.

CHAPTER 5
MY PRINCIPAL YEARS
1995 - 2005

In September of 1995, I was appointed Head Teacher of St. Peter's Primary School. Accepting the position at this time was extremely challenging, as the island was battered by two consecutive hurricanes and the school was badly damaged. I was faced with trying to manage a school that was damaged. It meant having to strategize how to arrange for the replacement of classrooms apart from being on the school's premises. It was a challenging time for me.

One of my first tasks upon assuming the role of principal was to create the school's crest and motto. The motto, "Rise and Achieve," was chosen because I realized that our students needed to be encouraged to climb the ladder of success. The crest was also designed with this in mind. It featured an eagle flying high with a book in its beak. The eagle signifies greatness, and the book signifies knowledge. I also composed the school song with the same theme in mind. The words to the song were put to music by Mr. Ian Hodge.

School Song

Oh, St. Peter's Primary School,
We commit ourselves and strive
To hold up our motto high
We will rise up and achieve.
Each day we'll do our best,
In Language Arts and the rest
We will hearken to our teachers
As they help us to achieve.
To reach the top is our aim,
As we strive for excellence
We will work hard and keep the rules of
St. Peter's Primary School.

Rising up and achieving was the guidepost of my tenure at the school. When the school was renamed in 2000, the words "St. Peter's" were replaced to enhance the new name, Deane-Glasford.

Another hallmark of my principalship was the renaming of St. Peter's Primary School to Deane-Glasford Primary School. This was done to honor two past educators at the school, Martha Deane and Doris Glasford. The renaming ceremony took place on January 8, 2000, at the school grounds. Mrs. Glasford returned home from Miami to participate in the renaming ceremony.

When I assumed the principalship of the school, I had a young staff. My words to them at that time were "It's all hands on deck. Together, we will raise the standard and create a successful school. Most of the teachers were new to teaching, and it was my responsibility to assist these teachers in achieving a high standard of teaching. To achieve this, I organized many staff development sessions that catered to training these teachers in classroom management, content teaching, and child development. In-house sessions were held weekly.

Teachers prepared lessons and executed them in the presence of all teachers. This was very productive as I watched teachers go out of their way to plan these lessons and execute them well. I took the opportunity to tell them that this level of preparation and execution must be done all the time in the classroom. As a result of this, there was an improvement in some areas of learning.

To address the weakness in the teaching of Mathematics, the school organized a Math Fair in 2001. Each class was responsible for a topic in Mathematics and designed teaching materials and strategies to help children learn that specific topic. This was very outstanding as teachers displayed very creative ways of teaching Mathematics. Parents came in their numbers to view this Math Fair. Hon. Timothy Harris, who was Minister of Education at that time, graced us with his presence. Ms. Carmen Ward, Education Officer, and Mr. Osmond Petty, who was the Math Professor at the Clarence Fitzroy College Teacher Division, were also in attendance. ZIZ TV also featured the activity on their newscast later that evening.

During my years as principal, the school achieved successes in sports, quiz competitions, and carnival activities. Our participants in the Rotaract Prince and Princess Show, Jermul Huggins and Aiden Nurse, won the crown that year. It was the first time that the school was successful in the competition. This was repeated the following year when Marvin Maynard and Monique Saddler represented the school. On both occasions, I wrote the dramatic piece, which was their talent performance. Our football team won the Interschool Primary School competition for the first time in 1996. The present President of the Football Association, Atiba Harris, was a member of that team.

Over the years, the school showed significant improvement in students who were placed in higher classes at Basseterre Junior High and later at the Washington Archibald High and Basseterre High School.

In 1999, we celebrated the 25th anniversary of the removal of the school from its old location at the St. Peter's Anglican Church to the present location in John England Village. The celebration was a tremendous success. The activities began with an Opening Ceremony, which was attended by the then Minister of Education, the Hon. Rupert Herbert. Activities also included an Anniversary Service at St. Peter's Anglican Church. For this service, past students were contacted. The response to this was phenomenal.

At the commencement of the service, each class from 1974 to 1999 was represented by three past students. One student carried the banner indicating the year, one carried a candle, and one spoke on behalf of the class. At this service, the message was brought by past student Ms. Ruthlyn Harris. The church was filled to capacity as many past students turned out in their numbers.

A walk-a-thon was another activity held as part of the 25th anniversary celebrations. It seemed as if the whole of St. Peter's turned out for this activity. Parents pushing strollers, older men and women, young and old, took the walk from the school to Frigate Bay. It was a tremendous success. The activities ended with an awards dinner in honor of Ms. Doris Glasford, who was the headmistress in 1974 when the school was relocated. This was held at the Ocean Terrace Inn. The guest speaker was Mr. Antonio

Christopher, a past teacher at the school. The then Prime Minister, Hon. Dr. Denzil Douglas, gave brief remarks.

At the end of these celebrations, I reflected on how well the community of St. Peter's supported the school, as attendance was outstanding. I capitalized on this and utilized members of the community at all events of the school.

Sadly, my time at Deane-Glasford came to an end in 2005. I was indeed sad to leave, but that season of my life ended abruptly, and I had to move on. My twenty-seven years in the St. Peter's community, serving first as a teacher and then as a principal, were challenging but extremely rewarding.

I am proud to know that I can now say St. Peter's Primary School/Deane-Glasford Primary has produced the present Prime Minister, Dr. Terrance Drew, as well as several doctors, nurses, teachers, construction workers, small business entrepreneurs, bankers, and civil servants. I am extremely pleased to see so many of them who have made an impact not only on the community of St. Peter's but on St. Kitts, as well as in various parts of the world. St. Peter's Primary/Deane-Glasford has come a long way, and I am glad I helped to shape the lives of so many students who attended the school.

I am happy to know that I helped to shape the minds of hundreds of students, change their lives, and inspire them to achieve. Each time I see or hear of their greatness, I can say they held up their motto high. They rose up and achieved

Not only did I teach in the elementary school, but my classroom was extended to the church. At the same time I became a teacher, I also taught Sunday school classes at the Zion Moravian Church. I taught Sunday School from 1974 to 1982. During that period, I also became a Warrant

Officer in the 1st St. Kitts Girls Brigade Company, also at the Zion Moravian Church. In 1985, I was commissioned as a Lieutenant in the same company and continued in that position until I immigrated to the United States in 2025.

While worshipping in Texas, I volunteered in the children's ministry at Christian Tabernacle from 2009 to 2019. The church changed its name and location in 2019, and I still volunteer at Inspire Church, the new location in Houston, Texas.

Both in the school and church, I have touched the lives of young children, and I am proud that my legacy is embedded in the lives of others.

CHAPTER 6
TEACHING IN TEXAS AT THE EARLY CHILDHOOD LEVEL 2009 - 2023

From 2005 to 2008, I resided in Tampa, Florida. In August of 2008, I relocated to Highlands, TX. I was unemployed and realized that without a bachelor's degree, I could not teach in an elementary school here in the United States. I eventually found employment at the John G. Jones Learning Center in Crosby, Texas, an early learning center. This was my first time teaching children ages 6 months to 4 years. I had no idea what this level of teaching entailed, but I gave it a try. Under the supervision of Ms. Agnes Hearon, the Director, I grew to like this line of work. I attended training sessions regularly, and it was at one of these training sessions that I discovered that I could pursue studies at San Jacinto College in Houston, Texas. I began to study for an Associate Degree in Education.

On the advice of one of the professors of the College, I was told that I should have my Trained Teachers Certificate from St. Kitts assessed to determine what its equivalent is here in the U.S. I did and discovered then that it was equivalent to an Associate Degree, so I discontinued those studies. I then applied to and was admitted to the Bachelor of

Science in Early Childhood at the University of Houston Clear Lake in 2009.

While pursuing these studies, I was told that I could not continue because I did not have an Early Childhood background. It was here that I experienced the work of God in my life. In the meeting, I told her I am not dropping from the program, but I will do whatever it takes to stay in. She advised me that I would have to attend classes at a community college in order to stay in the program. She outlined that I would have to do both studies, and it would be difficult to achieve. I told her I would pray about it. She said not even that would help me because it would be a momentous task.

With grit, determination, and prayer, I embraced the task. I worked at John G. Jones Learning Center in the daytime and attended night classes at both San Jacinto College, doing Early Childhood classes, and at the University of Houston Clear Lake to pursue a Bachelor of Applied Science in Early Childhood Education. This was a hard task, but I was determined to complete it, and with God's help, I graduated Cum Laude on Sunday, December 16, 2012. Interestingly, the professor who told me that it was a momentous task and I couldn't do it was on hand after my graduation to tell me what a great professional I was.

After graduating in 2012, I continued to work at John G. Jones Learning Center until August 31. I sought employment at the San Jacinto College Early Childhood Center in Houston as a Teaching Assistant and began work there on August 1, 2013. I worked there for one year, and on August 1, 2014, I began working with the Harris County Department of Education as a teacher at La Porte Head Start.

Head Start is a federally funded program in the United

States that provides free comprehensive early learning and development services to low-income children (birth to age 5 and their families. It aims to build school readiness through education, health, nutrition, and parent engagement.

My teaching experience at La Porte was challenging but fruitful. I enjoyed interacting with children ages 3 and 4 and worked with them using the Frog Street Curriculum. I enjoyed setting up my classrooms in the summer in preparation for the children's return in August. I enjoyed the home visits and Parent-Teacher conferences, as I interacted with the parents and got to know them better. Above all, I enjoyed working with these young children.

I enjoyed watching them display their creativity and communication skills in the Dramatic Play Center. I admired their creativity in Art. I watched them struggle to hold their crayons or pencils to write their names. I was amazed by their versatility and physical strength on the playground. I worked with them to identify the letters of the alphabet, as well as learning their numbers. Storytelling, rhymes, and singing were all part of the curriculum.

Teaching Head Start was a great experience for me. It taught me to study young children and embrace them for who they are. It was sometimes difficult, as they came in the morning to be calmed and prepared for the day's activities, but on most occasions, they would settle down. Some students suffered greatly from separation anxiety, and various methods had to be used to calm them and get them settled for the day. I helped children build their social skills by giving them opportunities to interact with their peers. Working with 3 and 4-year-olds was truly rewarding.

In 2018, I applied for and accepted the position of Assistant Campus Manager with the Harris County Department of Education. My assignment as ACM began at the J. D. Walker Head Start in Baytown, TX. As the Assistant Campus Manager, I was responsible for assisting the Manager, supervising the teachers with lessons, lesson plans, and classroom management. As ACM, I was the liaison between the teachers and the Coordinators at the Harris County Department of Education. This position gave me the ability to be in the classrooms and assess and evaluate what was taking place. I was able to keep abreast of what the children were doing and to give suggestions to the teachers for improvement.

Very early into my role as ACM, the Manager resigned, and I was entrusted with the task of being both the Manager and the Assistant Manager. A huge task indeed. I held this position from January 2019 to November 2019. In November 2019, Ms. Lisa Wells joined the staff as Campus Manager.

On July 31, 2023, I retired from teaching after spending 50 years in this career. My career, which started quietly and fearfully on Monday, October 1, 1973, ended quietly on July 31, 2023. A retirement program was organized by my Campus Manager, Ms. Lisa Wells, at the J.D. Walker Head Start. It was attended by my family, past and present co-workers. I felt A sense of accomplishment as I listened to their expressions of what I meant to those who were present.

I can truly say my living was not in vain. I was a teacher, I am a teacher, I will always be a teacher.

CHAPTER 7
MOTHERHOOD

On Thursday, July 16, 1981, I was joined in matrimony to Carl Samuel at the Zion Moravian Church, Basseterre, St. Kitts, supported by a large gathering of family and friends. Rev. Dufferin Culpepper was the officiating minister. A reception ceremony was held at the Factory Social Center.

This union produced three children. Carelle, my firstborn, was born in 1982. Carl Junior was born in 1985, and Cavaun was born in 1998.

When my sister migrated to the United States in 1990, I became the guardian of her three children, Trecia, Jamelle, and Yakim. Ably assisted by my mother, I cared for my two children at that time and my two nieces and nephew, giving me a total of five children.

They all attended the Victoria Road Pre-School in Basseterre and journeyed with me for their primary school education at the St. Peter's Primary School. These five bonded well together and became more like brothers and sisters to this day.

I kept them active in extracurricular activities and

encouraged them to take their education seriously. The boys were active in football, and the girls played netball at the primary school level. The girls took music lessons and were part of the liturgical dancers at the church. The girls were also members of the 1st St. Kitts Girls Brigade Company. The boys were members of the New Town Cub Scouts Pack.

Cavaun, who was born 13 years after his second sibling, actually grew up as an "only child," as they all migrated to the United States by the time he was five years old. He eventually moved with me to the United States in 2005, and together we lived first in Tampa, Florida, until 2009, when we moved to Highlands, Texas. He attended elementary school in Florida and Texas, and junior high and high school in Highlands, TX. In 2016, he moved to Prairie View, Texas, to attend Prairie View A & M University.

My niece Trecia holds a Doctor of Pharmacy from Florida A & M University in Tallahassee, Florida. My daughter Carelle holds a BA in Management and Administration from the City College of New York. My niece Jamelle works with a major airline in the United States, and both my son Carl Jr. and my nephew Yakim are entrepreneurs.

Along with my biological children, several of my past students call me "mommy" and actually refer to me as their mom. Three of those who are still connected with me to this day are Ayanna Hanley, Valencia Pemberton, and Lavita Harvey. Even though we are miles apart, I am kept abreast of their achievements, their struggles, and their lives as they unfold. I offer encouragement and guidance in times when they need it most. Two of those, Ayanna and Lavita, are teachers.

I can recall several parents reaching out to me to assist

them when they encountered difficulties dealing with their children. They would tell me, "Please help. He or she listens to you. Talk to him or her for me." Many years ago, one parent told me, "Please tell my child that, like you, I am a teacher, because every time I try to help him with his homework, he will say that's not how my teacher does it, and my teacher is right."

I feel blessed that my legacy is one of helping young children achieve success in life.

CHAPTER 8
POEMS WRITTEN BY MELVINA SAMUEL

FOR FIFTY YEARS OF SERVICE

For fifty years of service
Today we celebrate,
We're proud of our achievements.
The ranks of the Girls Brigade.
We hold up high our motto
Seek, serve, and follow Christ.
We honour our great Captain.
Jesus the crucified,

For fifty years of service
We wave our banner high,
To God we sing our praises
And thank Him for the past.
We look toward the future.
And know it will be bright.
For we will claim the promise
And go from strength to strength.

Written for the 50th Anniversary of the Girls Brigade Movement in St. Kitts in 2010.

GOD BLESS YOU, REV.

Our Pastor, brother, friend, and guide
We wish that you will forever here abide.
But nonetheless, we wish you well
As to others, God's Word you must tell.

Hungry and thirsty, faint and weak,
We came to you week after week,
Our hungry souls, you sure did feed.
And filled us up with what we need.

Humble, smiling, faithful, true.
You were called God's work to do.
And as today we honor you.
We know that God is pleased with you.

You laboured long, you laboured hard.
In this part of God's vineyard
And as you make another move.
You will more than conqueror prove.

God Bless you, Rev. We wish you well.
In our hearts, you'll forever dwell.
But we really have to let you know.
We just hate to see you go.

Poem written in July 2008 for the farewell service for Rev. Algernon Lewis of the Zion Moravian Church.

PREACH ON, O MAN OF GOD

Preach on, O Man of God
This church for you will pray,
That you'll continue in the faith
With God your guide each day.

You've been a stalwart here,
Igniting souls on fire
For Christ, you labored and inspired
You were our heart's desire.

You modeled well the young,
You inspired the old
Bright hope you brought to everyone
A shepherd to your fold.

Where'er your feet will trod,
You'll raise your banner high
A soldier for the Son of God
Victorious in the fight.

Preach on, O Man of God
Lay every burden down,
And when before our God you stand
He will bestow a crown.

Poem written and sang as a song to the tune of "Rise Up O Man of God" for the Farewell Service of Rev. Algernon Lewis of the Zion Moravian Church, July 2008.

PASTOR APPRECIATION

O Pastor, we appreciate you,
As the shepherd of this flock
You're so loving and so caring
As you lead us to the Rock
Oh what hope your preaching gives us
Oh what strength your praying gives us
You are truly blessed by God.

O Pastor, we appreciate you
May you go from strength to strength
May you never falter
As you preach from year to year
Then, when preaching days are over
And you lay the burden down
You will hear God say, dear Pastor
"Enter and receive your crown."

Poem written for Pastor Appreciation Sunday for Pastor Pamella Small.
All Nations in Love Ministry, Tampa, FL, April 2007.

POEM THE QUESTION MARK

Serenely perched upon a dot,
You set yourself into an inquisitive spot,
And oh! How very hard you try
Probing into what, when, where, and why?
You probe into what and how
Question Mark, take a bow.

You add much to the writing plot.
Like the seasoning in a pot.
You seek out answers from high and low
As thoughts and ideas quickly flow,
You make us search from deep within,
Then the answers all come in.

Poem written in 2010 as a writing assignment at the University of Houston-Clear Lake.

LOOK WHAT THE LORD HAS DONE!

God took my scar
And turned it into a star
For when all seemed lost and done
Look what the Lord has done!

"It's all over for you," the enemy laughed
As his strategy, he planned and drafted
But my God, with all power in his right arm
Proved that I can come to no harm.

I studied hard, I studied long.
Late at night or early morn.
Never faltering, having the end in mind
Now at last victory is mine.

Today I stand tall, dignified and proud,
"No weapon formed against me shall prosper," I shout.
"To God be the glory, to God be the praise,
Forever, I will praise His Holy Name."

Poem composed in December 2012 to commemorate my graduation from the University of Houston-Clear Lake with a Bachelor of Applied Science in Early Childhood Education.

MOMMA VIE

Hardworking, committed, humble, kind
Just these few words come to mind
Many were the sacrifices you made
Ensuring your children were top of the grade
You labored long, never complaining,
You labored hard and just kept on going.

Whether it was in the market or on the streets,
You sold your goods and did not retreat
In sun and rain, from morning 'til night
You went forth selling, all cheery and bright
Knowing that your children must be fed
And as you would say, I'm toiling for my daily bread.

Out of poverty you rose and stood tall,
And as a single mom, you did it all
You fed us, clothed us, and educated us
Always encouraging us to stay focused
You gave us all the tools we need.
And oh! how we did succeed,

With pride, you beamed at our successes
You helped to shape the skills we possess,
You charted our path, you paved the way
Your legacy lives on in us today,
Momma Vie, you are surely missed
Continue to rest in eternal bliss.

Poem in memory of my mother, Veronica "Momma Vie" Stevens.

REFLECTIONS

Slowly, I walked through the gate.
The year was nineteen seventy-eight.
I had made it to the school on the hill.
This school I had never seen before, located in Monkey Hill.
Confident, but with a lingering feeling of fear,
The question *"Why up there?"* kept ringing in my ears.

This was the question I heard from family and peers,
Anywhere else but not up there.
But there were smiles everywhere,
Friendly children, inquisitive, warm, and welcoming.
They seemed to say, *"We need you here."*
And so with that, I settled in.

Here I am at St. Peters Primary School.
I dug right in and pulled out my tools.
The classrooms were my workshops.
The children, my handiwork; I will never stop,
For I am here to impart knowledge and skill
To empower my students and values instill.

The work was hard, but I labored on
Year after year, never deterred, standing strong.
Teaching, coaching, supporting, loving,
Building character, inspiring, nurturing.
Teaching subjects, as well as respect and creativity.
Kindness, communication, and responsibility.

The year was nineteen ninety-five.
The call came loud and clear.
A principal is needed here
To help these children as they strive
To achieve their dreams and become intellectuals,
And motivate them in reaching their full potential.

With boldness, I answered the call
And issued the challenge to one and all.
I wrote the mission statement, motto, and song.
"Rise up and achieve" was our motto and our song.
To reach the top is our aim, for excellence we will strive.
Each boy, each girl must be inspired.

And now with pride I look and see,
Nurses, teachers, doctors, bankers, accountants.
Mechanics, pharmacists, contractors, masons, carpenters.
Engineers, clerks, farmers, footballers, entrepreneurs.
The list goes on and on in every profession.
And to top it all off, Dr. Drew, the Prime Minister

The year was two thousand – the turn of the century.
One fine sunny afternoon in January
At the school renaming ceremony
St. Peter's Primary now became Deane-Glasford
In honor of Martha Deane and Doris Glasford,
Two great teachers whose work must be remembered.

And now Deane Glasford Primary,
Let your light continue to shine in this community.
Greatness has come from among your walls,
I issue the call to teachers, parents, students, and all.

Continue to rise up and achieve!
And continue to build a lasting legacy.

Written in 2025 to launch my book entitled The Classroom.

ABOUT THE AUTHOR

Melvina Eldora Samuel, née Arthurton, always had a love for inspiring our nation's youth, and as such, on October 1, 1973, at the age of 17, she began her teaching career at St. Johnston Village School, currently known as Dr. William Connor Primary School. In 1978, Melvina completed her studies at the St. Kitts Teachers' College, graduating with a Trained Teachers' Certificate.

Upon graduation, Melvina was appointed as a trained teacher at St. Peter's Primary School, now called Deane-Glasford Primary School. With an effervescent thirst for knowledge, in 1989, Mrs. Samuel continued to pursue her studies in the field of education and received a Certificate in the Teaching of Reading from the University of the West Indies. She spent the rest of her teaching career at St. Peter's Primary School, having taught all grades ranging from kindergarten to grade 6, and was later appointed principal in September 1995.

Her first mission as principal was to make a request to the then parliamentary representative for a library that she believed would improve the reading abilities of the students and raise their literacy level. Mrs. Samuel played an imperative role in obtaining approval, and, as a result, the library was constructed and opened in 1997. As expected, the students continued to thrive and excel in their reading, which positively impacted the community.

In 2000, Mrs. Samuel also played an integral part in the

process of renaming St. Peter's Primary School to what it is now known as today, the Deane-Glasford Primary School. She is also the writer of the school's very first school song, "O Deane-Glasford Primary School," and the school's motto, "Rise Up and Achieve."

In 2005, Mrs. Samuel became ill and retired from her position at Deane-Glasford Primary School and migrated to the United States. In 2009, she pursued studies at the University of Clear Lake and graduated in December 2012 with a Bachelor of Applied Science in Early Childhood Education. During this time, she worked as a teacher at the John G. Jones Learning Center in Crosby, Texas, and as a teacher at the San Jacinto College Early Center in Houston, Texas. In 2014, she taught as a teacher with the Harris County Department of Education at La Porte Head Start, Texas.

In 2016, Mrs. Samuel graduated from the University of Clear Lake with a Master of Science degree in Early Childhood Education, and two years later, was appointed Assistant Campus Manager with the Harris County Department of Education at J. D. Walker Head Start in Baytown, Texas.

After a distinguished 50-year career in the field of education, nurturing young minds and inspiring countless others, Mrs. Samuel retired in July 2023, marking the end of a truly impactful tenure where she consistently demonstrated integrity, innovation, and creativity.

In November 2023, the Government of St. Kitts and Nevis awarded Mrs. Samuel with a Commander of the Star of Merit award for her dedication and years of service in the teaching profession.

She presently resides in Highlands, Texas. She has been married to Carl Samuel Sr for 44 years, and is the mother of three children, Carelle, Carl Jr., and Cavaun, and the grandmother of two girls, Carliyah and Faith.

Mrs. Samuel is grateful to God for the years she spent educating young minds. She has been a teacher to many, a mother to some, and an inspiration to all.

Made in the USA
Coppell, TX
21 February 2026

71953622R10039